ng

Ibi Lepscky

Leonardo da Vinci

Illustrated by Paolo Cardoni
Translated by Howard Rodger MacLean

BARRON'S

First paperback edition published 1992
by Barron's Educational Series, Inc.

First English language edition published 1984
by Barron's Educational Series, Inc.

All inquiries should be addressed to:
Barron's Educational Series, Inc.
250 Wireless Boulevard
Hauppauge, NY 11788

International Standard Book No. 0-8120-5512-8 (hardcover)
0-8120-1451-0 (paperback)

Library of Congress Catalog Card No. 84-342

Library of Congress Cataloging-in-Publication Data

Lepscky, Ibi.
  ₍Leonardo da Vinci. English₎
  Leonardo da Vinci / Ibi Lepscky; illustrated by
Paolo Cardoni; translated by Howard Rodger
MacLean. — 1st English language ed.

    p. cm. — (Famous people series)

  Cataloging based on CIP information.
  Translation from Italian.
  Summary: Describes the childhood of the
famous artist and inventor, whose early interests
in engineering, architecture, natural science, and
painting were encouraged by his father.
  ISBN 0-8120-5512-8 (hardcover)
          0-8120-1451-0 (paperback)

  1. Leonardo da Vinci, 1452–1519—Juvenile
literature. 2. Painters—Italy—Biography—
Juvenile literature. ₍1. Leonardo da Vinci,
1452–1519. 2. Artists 3. Inventors₎ I. Cardoni,
Paolo, ill. II. Title. III. Series.

₍ND623.L5L4413 1984₎   709'.2'4—dc19   84-342
                            ₍B₎ ₍92₎   AACR 2 MARC

                                                AC

PRINTED IN HONG KONG
2345 9927 987654321 (Paperback) (Hardcover) 2345 9927 98765

Leonardo

Leonardo was a very curious and bold little boy. Every day he would walk the countryside and look at things and ask questions.

Why did the rainbow have those wonderful colors?

Why did pebbles, thrown in a pond, make so many circles, which spread out and out and out?

And when he put twigs in the brook, where did the water carry them?

Leonardo's father was very proud of his son, who was always busy and had so many interests and so many imaginative ideas.

Leonardo lived in a village. His father worked in the city but often came to the village to see Leonardo. And every time he came, he wanted to know everything about his son and what he did.

One day he was told that Leonardo had done nothing but build. Using mud and stones, Leonardo had built a castle with very high towers. He had also built a small wooden bridge and a pinwheel that worked very well.

Leonardo's father was a notary and belonged to a family in which all the men, for over two hundred years, had been notaries. Notaries handled legal papers.

Watching Leonardo running with his pinwheel, his father thought, "I'm glad about this interest. Leonardo will become an engineer or perhaps an architect. He will break with this boring tradition of becoming a notary."

Very happy, Leonardo's father went back to the city and bought books on engineering, mechanics, and architecture. But when he returned to the village, people told him that his son hadn't built castles, bridges, or pinwheels for some time. Instead, he did nothing but study nature. He closely watched crickets and ants and other insects. He collected pebbles and sat for hours examining the form and pattern of flowers, leaves, and acorns.

"Perhaps I was wrong," his father thought, watching Leonardo spellbound by a beetle. "It appears Leonardo will become a scholar of the natural sciences. Yes, I think he will become a famous botanist or perhaps a geologist. He will break with this tiresome tradition of becoming a notary."

Very happy, Leonardo's father went back to the city and bought books on botany, natural sciences, and geology. But when he returned to the village, he was told that his son no longer studied insects, pebbles, and flowers. Instead, now he only drew. He drew everything he saw: farmers' tools, water jars, lambs,

olive trees, and straw bundles. He also drew large geometrical figures and ornamental designs.

"Perhaps I've been mistaken," his father thought, looking at Leonardo jumping in and out of large squares drawn in chalk on the ground. "Leonardo will become a painter. Yes, I'm sure he will. He will become a great painter and break this dull notary tradition."

Very happy, Leonardo's father went back to the city and bought paints, brushes, large sheets of paper, and books on geometry and ornamental design. But when he returned to the village, he was told that Leonardo had stopped drawing.

Instead, Leonardo was now interested in flying. He spent hours watching the way birds flew—how they flapped their wings, how they hovered with a beat of their tails, how they let themselves be carried by the air, how they glided back to earth.

Leonardo's interest in flying led to an interest in the air itself. He watched how the wind chased the clouds and how the leaves falling from the trees gently circled in the breeze.

Leonardo also made a large kite that flew high in the sky.

This time, however, his father felt discouraged.
"This child of mine is fickle," his father thought,
watching Leonardo running with the kite string in his
hand. "He starts a hundred things, and then he gets tired
of them. Perhaps Leonardo will end up becoming a notary
after all."

Very unhappy, Leonardo's father went back to the city. He was worried about his son. He did not know what would become of Leonardo.

But when he returned to the village again, people told him that his son was once again building castles, bridges, and pinwheels and that now, moreover, he had also built a windmill that worked perfectly.

They told him that Leonardo was once again watching insects, pebbles, flowers, and leaves and that now, moreover, he also studied larger animals—foxes, porcupines, and badgers.

He was told that Leonardo was once again drawing what he saw, as well as geometrical figures and ornamental designs and that now, moreover, he drew portraits of everyone he knew.

Leonardo's father also heard that his son was still interested in how birds flew and how the air behaved and that now, moreover, he wanted to fly himself. Leonardo had, in fact, made two large wings and launched himself from the roof of a barn. Luckily, he had fallen on a pile of straw without hurting himself.

Also, something new had happened. Leonardo now wanted to stay up at night to look at the planets, the stars, and the moon.

Leonardo's father suddenly understood that his son was not fickle and not half-hearted in his interests. Leonardo was, in fact, interested in everything and had an extraordinary ability for everything.

Leonardo grew up to become everything his father thought he would—engineer, architect, botanist, painter, inventor. He became all this and more, for Leonardo da Vinci was one of the greatest thinkers and creators of all time.